Rage

with Etiquette

Rhea L. Sholtis

BookLeaf
Publishing
India | USA | UK

I0191463

Copyright © Rhea L. Sholtis
All Rights Reserved.

This book has been self-published with all reasonable efforts taken to make the material error-free by the author. No part of this book shall be used, reproduced in any manner whatsoever without written permission from the author, except in the case of brief quotations embodied in critical articles and reviews.

The Author of this book is solely responsible and liable for its content including but not limited to the views, representations, descriptions, statements, information, opinions, and references ["Content"]. The Content of this book shall not constitute or be construed or deemed to reflect the opinion or expression of the Publisher or Editor. Neither the Publisher nor Editor endorse or approve the Content of this book or guarantee the reliability, accuracy, or completeness of the Content published herein and do not make any representations or warranties of any kind, express or implied, including but not limited to the implied warranties of merchantability, fitness for a particular purpose.

The Publisher and Editor shall not be liable whatsoever...

Copyright © 2021 ...

All rights reserved.

Dedication

For the daughters who learned silence to survive and for the mothers who taught it out of love, believing it was the only way life could be kind.

To my husband, **Tom**, who held me through every unlearning.

Preface

These poems were born in the moments I refused to shrink.

This collection moves past simple rage to explore the clarity that fury can forge. It is, at its heart, my love letter to women going through the journey: **Inheritance, Eruption, and Reclamation**—a necessary return to power after imposed limitations.

If you find yourself raw, trembling, furious, or forgiving within these pages... know this one truth as you read: **You were never too much.**

Acknowledgements

To my **mother,** whose inner strength forms the very
bones of these pages.

To my sister, **Rose June,** whose keen eye gave this work
its final polish.

To my husband, **Tom,** whose unwavering belief made
this book a reality; it carries your steadiness in its spine.

To my friends, **Allain, Annie May, and Myrtle Dawn,**
thanks for the low-maintenance friendship across the
distance and the book cover feedback.

To the **Vargas-Locsin families and friends,** thanks for
giving me the space to be both my complicated self and a
"Rhea of sunshine."

To **Vito's Tea House in Uniontown, PA,** where the
promise of this collection was made.

And finally, to the **readers**—may these poems remind you
that to burn beautifully is always your true nature,

Maraming Salamat.

1. Inheritance of Quiet Women

My mother swallowed storms
and bit down on thunder.
I learned to hum through typhoons.

Calloused, uncomplaining hands
fed the world
while her own hunger
went unnamed.

She carried her ache
like a hidden altar,
a history her children
were never allowed to read.

She bent like bamboo,
praying only that the wind
would spare her roots.

I carry that same quiet now.
Silence, I've learned, is not peace.
It's survival.
Inherited.

2. The Weight of Stillness

Stillness has bones.
I can feel them
press against my ribs when I hold my breath
too long.

Every time I bite my tongue,
the air thickens.
A pause grows heavy
until it becomes a bruise.

They say patience is a virtue—
but they've never waited
with a locked jaw.

Stillness is a load-bearing wall.
And I've been its foundation for far too long.

3. To My Mother, Milagros

I wanted to ask
if you ever screamed underwater,
just to keep the sound from reaching anyone.

You taught me to pray.
Quietly.
To fold anger like laundry:
neat, hidden,
smelling faintly of soap and surrender.

I believed control was required.

If you could hear me now,
I'd confess:
I broke the pattern.
And the world didn't end.

4. House Rules (Rewritten)

Original taped to the fridge:
Don't answer back. Don't raise your voice. Be grateful.

New version written in red lipstick on my mirror:
Ask why. Speak when it matters. Volume is not violence.

And beneath these handwritten words,
a reflection
of the woman
who **finally** rewrote them.

I keep both copies.
One for memory.
One for mercy.

5. The Slow Undoing

They taught her meekness like scripture.
A Sunday hymn she mouthed daily under her breath.

They sold her compliance as power
but she learned power does not wait to be granted.

They convinced her that kindness keeps her protected,
but it only kept her from hearing herself.

So, she began the slow undoing.
thread by thread,
rule by rule.

Unlearning how to fold herself small,
and claiming what was always hers.

6. Ang Bait Mo (You Are Kind)

They said, *"Ang bait mo."*

And she was.
A soft voice, steady hands.
Quick to stand, to serve, to smile.

She learned early that her worth
was measured in how eagerly she helped.

There's grace in that:
The way she kept others whole,
even while she was **unraveling.**

But kindness, stretched too thin,
becomes absence.
And even deities
get tired of being thanked.

She's just now learning the difference
between good and gone.

She still sets the table
but sometimes she sits down first.

And when they say, *"Ang bait mo."*
She smiles again,
not out of duty this time,
but recognition.
Because she is—
just not for the same reasons anymore.

7. Sorry, Out of Habit

She used to begin every sentence with *"Sorry."*

Sorry for asking.
Sorry for taking space.
Sorry for the quiet
after overexplaining.

It was habit,
like smoothing a tablecloth
no one noticed was wrinkled.

They told her humility was grace.
But she had seen grace
used like a leash.

So, she gathered **every apology
she never owed**
and let them fall
without ceremony.

No fanfare.
Just a woman
returning her borrowed guilt.

And when they wait
for her to shrink again,
she lets the **air stretch**...
beautiful and earned.

8. Politeness Fatigue

She's tired of smiling
under fluorescent lights,
of small talk echoing
in concrete halls,
of holding elevator doors
for people who never look up.

Her voice used to blend with traffic honking,
chatter,
the drone of too much doing.
Now she lets silence
cut through the static,
a clean line of disobedience.

She has seen that gentleness
can bruise.
That poise gets heavy
when the city won't stop moving.

So, she slips her phone to silent,
lets messages pile like litter,
and watches her reflection
in the glass window—
a woman still,
while the world keeps rushing.

Even warmth needs distance.
Even light
has limits.

9. Permission Revoked

She spent her lifetime saying yes
to keep the commune
that never kept her.

This first time wasn't loud.
It didn't need to be.
Just a **breath**,
a single syllable
that stopped the chatter.

She said *no*
and meant it,
not as a refusal,
but as arrival.

And the room held its breath.
not out of anger,
just **surprise**
that she didn't flinch this time.

No apology, no trembling.
Only the clean sound
of her own boundary
closing gently
around her.

10. The Space Between Saints and Sins

The angels taught her patience.
The demons, momentum.

Caught between devotion and desire,
she stopped asking who was right,
and started taking notes.

The angels said, "*Ensure.*"
The demons said, "*Enjoy.*"
Both wanted worship.
Neither offered peace.

So she stood in the limbo,
a living boundary.
Her skin, a live wire of contradiction.

The angels offered mercy.
The demons, understanding.
She took both and owed nothing.

She studies distance
as self-possession.
How far she must stand
to heal herself again.
Some holiness, she has learned,
is just another kind of hunger.

11. She Burns Neatly

They used to call her purest ore,
The kind of core you must explore.
They never felt the rising fire,
Nor the embers fueled by deep desire.

No spark, no flame leapt to the sight,
But a steady, unyielding, piercing light.
Her being was the vessel they did not know,
The silent mastery they watched grow.

She learned to burn with measure and art,
To scorch but leave no ruined part.
No scar, no shout, no broken wall,
But truth refined that stands up tall.

Now everything she touches bears the strain,
The terrible elegance she shows in pain.
No rage, no clamor, no need for grief,
Strategy is her cruel relief.

12. Controlled Chaos in Silk Gloves

She learned subtlety from fire.
How to burn quietly,
how to destroy without leaving smoke.

Her repose unnerves them more
than fury ever could.
It's the inhale before the match is struck.

Once, she bit her tongue
until she tasted iron.
Today her rage is curated, soft-spoken,
wearing pearls and precision.

Every movement measured,
wrapped in rose perfume.

She doesn't raise her voice anymore.
She just tilts her head,
and the stage remembers
what power looks like
when it no longer explains itself.

13. Fluent in Restraint

The abyss bends around her,
not from force,
but focus.

She doesn't fill space.
She defines it.

Slight gestures
that shift
the air's direction.

No saints here,
no sinners either.
Only bodies knowing
where not to stand.

She doesn't carry brimstone,
she carries stillness,
Tuned to the pitch
before the glass shatters.

Every word she speaks
lands exactly
where she meant it
to be known.

And when she smiles,
it's not a softness.
it's an understanding.

The world,
finally fluent
in her restraint.

14. The Silent One

They say silence is weakness.
As if quiet doesn't KILL.
As if graves aren't FILLED with the ones
who thought silence was SAFE.

So, I let them talk.
Stacking their little victories
on bricks I laid in the shadows.
I watched them climb higher,
never seeing the ground already CRACKING.

I don't want applause.
Not for the FIRE I fed.
Not for the shoulders I gave
until they SPLINTERED.

But when silence breaks,
when my ENOUGH hits like THUNDER in their chests,
they'll learn quiet is not harmless.

It's patience strung taut as a bow.
A blade waiting for release.
And when it CUTS, they'll bleed
before they even know they're open.

So, judge the quiet—the cutting!
Judge this WOMAN WHO WALKS AWAY
while the walls FALL behind her.

They expected a DRIZZLE,
a sky too timid to weep.
But what they got was a TEMPEST,
one that chewed through bone
and left NOTHING standing.

Because STORMS don't write eulogies.
They ERASE them.
Leaving a SILENCE so loud,
it BURIES the living.

15. Inheritance Honored

My mother whispered fortitude.
I commanded pause.

What was unyielding
I have learned to relent by choice.
What was meek persistence
I have learned to make my voice.

My mother folded storms
to hide the ache.
I unbend her sheath
to drive in my stake.

No master left.
Only the bone-deep truth of self.
No myths to defend.
Only the clear space on the shelf.

I keep the tallow,
the slow. unanchored gleam of it.
I change the story
with the fierce, thrumming heart of it.

The ancestry remains
but the narrative shifts.
A legacy reclaimed,
as the mending begins.

16. The Whole Name

For years
they said her name wrong
and she let them.

She shortened it,
softened it,
cut it into small pieces
so it would fit
in their mouths.

But now. She speaks it whole.

Each syllable strikes
like a hammer,
like an oath,
like a verdict.

Her name no longer asks
to be remembered.

It insists.
It demands to be repeated
and they feel it.

The weight.
The warning.
The woman.

17. Do Not Trespass

She did not burn the map
they had given her.
She needed to know the terrain
she was finally leaving.

She took a pen.
A sure, deliberate instrument,
And on the center where the **X** used to mark,
she left one single instruction:

<u>DO NOT TRESPASS.</u>

Her border became the only mandate of the land.

She pocketed the paper
not to hide it, but to hold it.
A private deed of ownership.

18. The Unmaking

They all believed that healing
meant putting herself back together.
She disagreed.

She said,
What if I like the gaps?
What if I earned the space
between what I was,
and what I became?

She said,
What if I stop
trying to mimic the shape
they remember?
Until there's nothing left
that truly doesn't belong to me.

Because maybe I'm not broken.
Maybe I'm rearranged.

Let them call it what they want.
Names are for things
that stay still.
And I don't.

This is her birthright.

To unmake.
To unbecome.
To unfold.

19. Only Order

They ask for a receipt! They demand an inventory!
They want to know what I packed and what I threw
away!
But I have reached the final decree of my own country:
To refuse to explain what I keep.

The world doesn't test me now.
The world doesn't fight me now.
The world doesn't break me now.
There is only order.
A brutal, absolute, shining order.

No panic. No shaking. No plea.
Hands steady.
Heart measured.
I am moving through the rubble of the person I used to
be.
Moving through what's left.
Like a mason on the final day.
Setting the capstone for a tower that will never, ever
sway.

Listen: There is no comfort here.

There is no respite in it.

Respite is for the soft, the searching, the undecided.

I am beyond that need.

You see the empty space? You see the great, yawning hole?

The thing that should consume me? The thing that should take my soul?

The Void trails behind me.

It is a shadow. It is a companion.

I took the emptiness and wove it with my faith.

I taught the nothingness its place.

It is devoted.

It is hers.

It. Is. Mine.

20. The Small Hours

The house is still,
but not asleep.

Dawn gathers at her feet,
thin as
resolve.

Steam from the cup
spins the air,
like mettle
learning how to rise.

The daybreak outside's
still inventing its noise.
But here,
everything moves
to her beat.

This is what truth looks like
when it belongs
to no one else.

21. The Ocean Doesn't Waste Itself

Someone once asked her
"What's your secret?"

She smiled, slow as tide,
And the light moved closer to listen.

"I stopped chasing puddles", she said,
"and offering my storms
to those who only wanted rain.

Stopped folding my depth
to fit the shallow.
Stopped explaining the vastness
that keeps me whole

Now I choose the deep,
the pull that teaches surrender,
the dark that mirrors truth,
the current that feeds her.

The day I gave up puddles
I became the sea itself."

The ocean
doesn't waste its essence
on ripples.

She remembers every woman who refuses to drown.

www.ingramcontent.com/pod-product-compliance
Lightning Source LLC
Chambersburg PA
CBHW050955030426
42339CB00007B/397

* 9 7 8 1 8 0 7 1 5 3 1 3 7 *